Secrets for Influencers:

Growth Hacks for Tik Tok

Table of contents

Complete guide to gain followers and monetize Tik Tok

One of the social networks with the greatest impact today is Tik Tok, since 2019 its popularity has not stopped growing, even surpassed all kinds of expectations, this platform is made up of a youthful target dedicated to teenagers, since 80% of users are between 13 and 25 years old.

The reach of this social network has caused it to become the target of many influencers, for this reason if you are looking to build a great presence and get followers, you need to know in depth everything behind this social network so you can undertake in style.

Discover every detail of Tik Tok

The possibility of personal growth in Tik Tok is in your hands, it is a social network dedicated to videos that has become one of the most downloaded, so nowadays it is a great need to get more knowledge to explore all the possibilities when sharing original content.

The use of this social network is available for both Android and IOS, allowing a wide network of active users, who can enjoy and share 15 or 60 seconds maximum of videos, its dynamics is based on a fusion between Instagram stories along with Snapchat.

In the middle of this social network there is a wide catalog of free license audio and music so that the videos can receive this type of animation, in addition to this is available the option to integrate your own audio and share them so that other users can use them on their videos.

Normally the essence of this social network is based on dubbing and all kinds of scenes, there is no limit to commemorate the scene you want with the advantages of this application, all thanks to the functions that arise through artificial intelligence, to start enjoying the ways of recording.

There are two ways to record in Tik Tok, the first is from the application itself, so that you can then open the way to integrate all kinds of effects, on the other hand you can also make the recording from another application to upload the video from your own gallery.

Creativity is not limited thanks to the large number of effects that can be used on the videos, such as masks, transitions and sounds, in addition to the use of hashtags, where visibility is gained so that the content can reach more users, which is why it is a medium dedicated to entertainment.

What kind of videos can be uploaded to Tik Tok?

The basis of Tik Tok videos are based on the use of filters, effects and other tools that the application itself provides, that is why there is such a variety of original content, everyone can add their own touch to record videos and among the most popular recording styles are the following:

Playback

The modality of this video is to perform the interpretation of an existing audio within this application, where the dynamics is carried out with a great action of gesticulating every aspect that is related to the audio, so that it seems that you are the one who sings, this type of video has a great popularity.

Duet

A feature that Tik Tok provides and is widely used is the action of duets, with another user you can create content, all you have to do is select the video of the other user, to record the video reacting to the one you have chosen, that way both videos will appear on the screen at the same time.

Slow-motion

Through this kind of video you get a great alternative well known about teenagers, the effect is to record in slow motion, this is coupled with the audio that is ideal for that type of recording, this is a recording option a little complex, so Tik Tok values them in the recommended page.

Interpretation

There are many types of performance videos on Tik Tok, the ones that cause the best visibility on the social network are the comical ones, either through a joke or a made-up story, the important thing is that the narration can be done in an exaggerated way so that kind of charisma can hook others.

Tricks / teaching

The Tik Tok community is passionate about learning, so to rise above the competition this is an optimal way, where you can quickly explain about a topic while keeping the role entertaining, it is ideal for sharing recipes and also to generate a review on a favorite movie.

The popularity of Tik Tok

The attention that a social network like Tik Tok provides is based on its focus on everything that interests you, its operation is completely extended to focus on the favorites section, giving users the advantage of getting rid of content that is not pleasant.

The powers of Tik Tok allow you to select the "Not interested" option for a long time, thus sending a direct signal that you no longer want to come across this type of content.

However, the options do not stop, because you can hide some kind of specific content, so that what is outside your interests can not become annoying, although this is added to the consideration that by limiting and optimizing the experience on the social network this influences the sequence of your videos.

The usefulness of Tik Tok in your content marketing

All the milestones that Tik Tok has surpassed are postulated as important reasons to be passionate about trying some advertising objective on the platform, as the groups and audience is a brilliant opportunity to postulate your aspirations to grow, because you will be able to reach all types of customers regardless of country or business.

It is not a simple fashion platform, but it is a massive media that is suitable for all types of brands, so you can enter any home, social group, there is no limit, on the other hand there are certain ad formats that work as a great increase of interaction.

Every social media marketing effort fits with Tik Tok, even for B2B, this social network has a huge appeal, especially if your target audience is present on Tik Tok, to interact in a real way and present your industry topic in a more creative way.

Integrating video to any commercial claim is a must, especially for your business to become an influential media, where the product or service can be shown using it in real life, this is a great opportunity to advertise in style, achieving a user base with dynamics and tools.

Tik Tok for companies and its advantages

The power that Tik Tok has generated breaks with any scheme, that is why it is a target for many companies because they can reach that large number of users who keep using the application several times a day, with its usage metrics it becomes a first level metric compared to other social networks.

The option to humanize a commercial intention through this social network is a reality, especially because of the high level of engagement you can get thanks to the content created, since the organic reach is of the highest level to reach far regardless of the small number of followers you have.

It is very easy to generate a viral video with this platform, especially where the views and interaction are guaranteed, in addition to undertaking a new account is rewarded by the application, it is very noticeable the power that arises from this platform for a brand to grow.

The creation of videos should be fun and this helps to motivate in a clear way any commercial pretension, also you can broadcast courses and all kinds of activities that generate great interaction, that kind of presence is a more friendly tone to gain attractiveness, to this is added the opportunity to integrate content marketing.

Tik Tok PRO (analytics)

The PRO account type in Tik Tok is a modality that very few get to know, it is a special offer for influencers, bloggers and also for brands, thanks to the fact that it provides detailed information about the statistics that you present within the application, so you can measure your progress.

By using this type of data you can focus on improving and understanding the strength of the type of content you share, this type of insight is a great opportunity to track growth within this platform, it becomes easier to achieve the popularity you crave by knowing how to do it.

Once you set up your account, and you have defined a category type, you can closely follow the direct analytics on the account, both visits and subscribers, the content is also studied by seeing the likes, visits and audience, in addition to the option to advertise in the application.

With this kind of information from the application, you can perform an exhaustive analysis, to not lose step towards that competitive account you need so much, you can also develop advertising strategies dedicated to this data, statistics are displayed to evaluate performance more clearly.

Popularity dynamics are added as another data that you can easily see, thus showing the impact that your content is having, in addition to the understanding that arises to design a better image to the target audience, it is a better definition of what you want and what you are looking for.

Once you can have a PRO account to use it to the fullest you can keep publishing or sharing content that is ideal for your brand, i.e. creating content that provides news about the sector or category you work in, as well as tips since the community is very attentive to learn.

On the other hand, you can not lose sight of the stories to humanize, with empathy you can strengthen better ties with the community, the type of content that causes better reception is the short, especially if they are tutorials, to value time and simplicity, the important thing is to be understood.

Once you manage to arouse curiosity about your brand, there is no doubt that you will have a large following, and you can offer constant challenges so that they do not detach from your account, remember that this is an entertainment platform so the value you should look for is towards that area.

Tik Tok challenges dedicated to companies

Given the high number of downloads that Tik Tok has gene-rated in a short time, it is a social network that invites a large flow of interaction on a daily basis and is therefore valuable for a company, although the question of how to improve the exposure of a brand in Tik Tok has surely arisen, this means taking on a clear challenge.

You can use the challenges of Tik Tok to your advantage to grow within the digital environment, although it is still a fertile and in-production environment as far as advertising is con-cerned, but a wealth of opportunities sprout up for brands to reach another size class up to a top-tier campaign.

The challenges of Tik Tok are shaped by the broad meme culture, as it is content as a result of social media marketing, so more and more brands are joining a trend using this form of expression or content, this combination of text and images has another value in Tik Tok.

Video memes become a better dynamic, so as not to lose the entertainment over any commercial message, so the cha-llenge for a company is to unite their goals along with text, sound and movement that serves as a kind of performance.

This is the way for a commercial project to be the protagonist within this social network, therefore it is an obligation for a brand to start investing by setting an advertising plan on this social media, in a digital era dominated by the special ability of the content that is shared on the internet is a great opportunity to explore.

Within Tik Tok there are a great number of alternatives for the commercial purpose to obtain the reach you desire, where customized sounds can be used in your favor to generate a great impression and reach each one of the users that use this application.

In order to find the ideal impact within Tik Tok it is an absolute must to attend to every organic measure to be attentive to those pushes that translate into a large number of followers and above all interaction, thus your video becomes an opportunity to grow a business or any other goal.

There are three ways to find the challenge that is most compatible with your brand:

Search the For You page

This is a complete exploration on For You to find a lot of suggestions linked to the content that you can enjoy, this section is very variable as you start following accounts, this is an area similar to the "Explore" page that Instagram has, it is important to take close care of this aspect.

It is important to make sure you follow influencers that are part of Tik Tok and that are related to your content, so you can identify the type of content that is published and can be used as inspiration, the important thing is to have the power to recreate in your account the best slant for commercial intent.

Keep track of trending sounds

This is an ideal way to get inspired in the action of finding trending challenges, because the selection of sounds that belong to Tik Tok as they are a reflection of the subject matter that has the most power online, by tapping or pressing on a sound you can see the videos that have originated based on these sounds.

By paying full attention to the most useful sounds, along with the movements that go into the creation of the video, you can gain a greater incentive for inspiration in every way, these tricks are a great start so that the editing can follow the expected commercial course.

Understand Tik Tok compilations on YouTube

On YouTube you can find a lot of stars that convey to users a lot of weird and novel challenges that you can put into action, that way you don't lose sight of recent concepts, that's why some good Tik Tok compilations serve as a great inspiration for you.

When looking for real content, it is important to perform advanced searches, this also helps you save time and when you have clearer ideas that are related to your brand, you only have to inquire about the most convenient and advise you about it.

Learn how to undertake a Tik Tok challenge campaign

When faced with the idea or the desire to create a challenge campaign in Tik Tok, the most crucial thing is the context, in addition to the ease and diversity of memes to create a quality video, since there are many aspects to find the right inclination such as the effects and also the possibility of including real sounds.

The main thing is to know the type of commercial purpose you are looking to promote, then think of a music related or that can be associated with that sector, to move on to make a list with the background and the best recreation to emit a nostalgic effect on users and the audience.

The steps to follow so that a campaign can be consolidated in Tik Tok and that your commercial purpose is authentic are the following:

Plan the type of campaign to be undertaken

It is important that you can plan a challenge campaign that is attached to your brand, that is the main objective of all a dedication, in this way your target market gets to know that it exists as a commercial proposal, but for this the contribution of a large number of followers serve as a great presentation. To boost sales in a great way, you should always think about how to link the product or service to the interaction that Tik Tok postulates, so the measure of defining the main objective of any campaign is a basic but forceful step, for this you must also track online trends.

To work with Tik Tok you can rely on the power of Google Analytics, that way you can promote great content and manage to spread a greater appeal on the masses, at this point is when it becomes more important to execute a first level marketing campaign, that is the approach that can not be lost.

Visualize the shaping of a challenge as if it were a competition, this is a method of participation in the digital world that cannot be lost, this culture is one of the most important to learn so that the aspirations of building a versatile and modern brand are not left aside.

Plan Tik Tok challenge content

Taking into account the importance of Tik Tok and the objectives that can be established to grow through this social network, the next thing to do is to tell a story that is entertaining, so that it can be broadcasted in the video and generate that letter of introduction by the commercial intention.

To grow quickly online it is essential to create something special, that way the attraction cannot be lost for any reason, although it cannot be so complicated to keep replicating online, otherwise the target audience will not be able to join the challenge and the intention is for each follower to broadcast it to their followers.

As long as the challenge can sweep the interest of all, it will generate a large organic flow difficult to ignore by the followers, that is the link with social networks that will cause the brand can get a very important level, for this reason as long as you can analyze the content better fate will acquire.

Choose an appropriate sound in Tik Tok

The sound to be used on the Tik Tok challenge must be well studied and above all is to opt for an original sound, this element is basic for each video can be issued with the importance it deserves, for the selection should be selected films, and viral videos to find phrases that relate to your industry.

Choreograph each step for the challenge

Whether by means of professional support or your own creativity, it is important to define the star of the video and the type of recreation to be captured, in addition to defining the level of difficulty, the important thing is not to lose creativity, but to move people so that the video can reach more people.

Create and share the Tik Tok challenge

By covering each of the movements, sounds and the context of the challenge, everything is completely ready for the recording to take place, it is best to take the proper time to cover each of these steps accordingly, the important thing is that it is a perfect end result that is worth it.

It is important to feel satisfaction with the realization of the video, for this you can choose the best editing resources, it is a masterpiece in every way, so that it can relate to other people and every digital corner, constitute drafts and seek marketing advice to attract a large audience.

Facts you should know about Tik Tok

In the midst of the development of Tik Tok's functions, there is a great variety of data that are useful for you to grow within this platform as every user wishes, in this sense, the following stand out:

The application in its country of origin (China), does not have the name or denomination of Tik Tok, but is known as "Douyin", which means shake music in Mandarin.

The application meets a launch dating back to about 2016, and in record time in 2019 surpassed the popularity of downloads compared to Facebook, YouTube, Instagram and Snapchat.

Most of the users of this platform are teenagers, which is a quality of the target audience, although there is also a 27% of people between 30 and 40 years old that can be taken advantage of.

In India the downloading of this application is prohibited and restricted due to security issues, it is a restriction due to cultural issues.

The average user spends 52 minutes a day on the application, and logs on up to 7 times within that time frame.

Tik Tok's growth potential is idea for all kinds of marketing strategies, especially with the reach of the eager target audience.

Every day up to one million videos are viewed on this social network so it is a constant movement.

The purpose within this social network changes compared to other platforms, as it is a fast and interactive work, because it is a much more dynamic content.

This social network has a global posture as it is available in 155 countries, so it is designed in 75 languages, being a potential niche to carry out any strategy.

The value of this social network is postulated at over 75 billion dollars.

This platform has modalities such as a "Pro" account, which allows you to have contact with a data analysis to seek greater effectiveness within this platform and deliver the content or growth you aspire.

How the Tik Tok feed is formed

Managing content properly in Tik Tok is relevant to the algo-rithm, especially because an account must have a high per-formance for each video to get more views, and this does not have to do only with the number of followers as it is thought, the key is to customize each section of content.

This usually brings huge doubts for people who are new and have not yet interacted with content, so what you should do is select categories that are of interest, these are varied so that they can fit with your goals, they can be pets, or any other kind of theme you have in mind.

The information you provide to the platform is your best sup-port to create a high level initial feed, by polishing these as-pects and recommendations that is used as a starting point to gain interaction on the first videos you publish, as long as they are frequent and comply with advertising actions.

When you do not select a favorite category, the social net-work itself is responsible for providing a general source of popular videos, so from now on when some kind of interac-tion arises, it becomes a basis for the system it uses to de-termine your interests and make content suggestions.

The interaction you can post on this social network at the beginning for others to find you is to follow accounts, visualize the hashtags of your interest, know each of the sounds and effects, to get into the trending topics just go to "Discover" so that the user experience generates a flow of action.

By performing these actions on the feed, you set the Tik Tok algorithm to work in your favor, so that when a user tries to find a video that is not part of their target, it is only discarded so that you can set your preferences comfortably.

The real gem of Tik Tok is also about the ease of promoting a commercial intent or other type of digital site, and this also works the other way around, that's why on Instagram you can link your account without any problem, plus you can also get a web link, being a great funnel offering.

You can create a video with a commercial message and hope that it becomes a viral theme, all thanks to the fact that viewers will be able to visit your profile and get followers or any other action that raises interest, achieving the purchase you expect, so it is essential to optimize the biography.

The call to action to your content, arises through the profile, that way you can comfortably aspire to the desired conversion occurs, where the appearance and activity of the account will be responsible for speaking, this is an essential step before entering into the other details of each publication or broadcast.

In the same way that you take care of your Instagram or Twitter bios, in the same way you have to use every Tik Tok choice to climb towards a higher user preference, this kind of integrated elements become an important attention grabber that becomes irresistible.

The comparison between Tik Tok and Instagram

The similarity of content and interaction between Tik Tok and Instagram, generates big questions about which social network option is much more feasible in terms of recreation and shopping, the point of comparison arises with the stories, but in Tik Tok they do not expire in 24 hours as happens with Instagram.

The real similarity of Tik Tok is with YouTube, mainly because of the possibility of creating and publishing content, although in the case of the algorithm of the second social network is a little late and the video may not generate the effect you expect, much less in the way you want.

The important thing is that the videos do not disappear, this is a power to continue looking to gain a little more traffic, even months after having published the content, giving a great opportunity for people with few followers to climb to get thousands of visits even.

Tik Tok is much more than an application to make videos, it has become a genuine social network, where the opportunity to earn money arises, so it is a great attraction for many companies, and at the same time an environment of growth for an influencer, likewise the presence in these media is important.

After the application received some threats, it was presented the launch of an Instagram function similar to Tik Tok, but the strong side of this application is still latent by the power to create and edit videos to issue results of real interaction, especially for being a brief and charismatic content.

Instagram, on the other hand, has a focus on aesthetics, then it grew with the integration of stories, until extending the possibilities of actions, until Instagram TV is presented, where video content reaches 60 seconds, although it only accepts pre-recorded content until the launch of reels.

The video editing that is presented on this function is important, it is a competition that seeks to take great similarity with

Tik Tok, as you can create 15-second videos, these clips can be formed by being recorded or added from the gallery, from this creation you can make all kinds of effects, its function is very easy.

Tik Tok has the function to share your videos on Instagram, through reels the whole process becomes much easier than you think, so the content can be installed on Instagram to gain more attraction, and even raise the number of followers, it is a great power to have both platforms.

Tik Tok search and find tricks

Once you can fully associate yourself with the features of Tik Tok you can find much broader options for you to find and broadcast the content you want within this application, the answers you need are as follows:

Search and find a Tik Tok video

A basic way to find a video happens in a basic way by looking at the home screen, then you can go to the following steps:

1. Access Startup through the menu bar.

2. Then by tapping on the menu you can see at the top the videos of all the accounts you are following.

3. Once the videos are exposed, you only have to play the ones that are part of the trend or the recommendations that are of your preference.

Another way to access is through Discover, this is done through the following steps:

1. The main thing to do is to go to Discover via the menu bar.

2. You can select the video that appears above the carousels of hashtags that are part of the trend and also at the top you can search for them.

The third way to find a video, is to go to the ones that have been marked as favorites or any that you have liked, by means of these actions:

1. Enter "My" through the menu bar.

2. Click on the bookmark icon to watch the videos you have bookmarked or save as a viewing option for later.

3. You can also re-enter the videos you have liked by going to the section headed by a heart icon.

When you find the video, you can have the freedom to perform the interaction you want, you can even react to perform some kind of duet, or even create a live photo, since Tik Tok has a lot of alternatives, but apart from its valuable options you can find videos through sound or using the hashtags of your interest.

Search and find videos by sound on Tik Tok

If you want to view or be inspired by videos that use a specific audio clip, you can perform this type of search by filtering the sound as a priority, this becomes a reality after the following step-by-step:

1. Search and select the video you are interested in with the particular sound.
2. Click on the sound link at the bottom of the video.
3. Once from the sound page that pops up, you can add the sound to your favorites, share it, and even find the original usage if available, to start recording a video using that sound if you wish.

Another alternative to this need is that you can find sounds by searching on the screen under "Discover".

Search and find videos by effects on Tik Tok

To see many more videos that are using this effect, you only need to follow these steps:

1. Find a video that has the effect of your interest.

2. Click on the effect that appears with a wand over the video creator.

3. The above action takes you to the page of the effect you are looking for, so you can add this option to your favorites, that way you can share it as you wish, even start recording using it.

On the other hand, you can also find the effects by searching through the screen under the "Discover" option.

Search and find videos by hashtags on Tik Tok

If you want to watch more videos tagged with hashtags, you should follow these guidelines:

1. Search for a video that has a hashtag that interests you.

2. Click on the hashtag above the title at the bottom of the video, where the creator of the video is identified.

3. When you are on the hashtag page that appears after clicking, you can add the one you find ideal for your pretensions, then you can share and find other kinds of videos that use this kind of tags, up to being able to record a new video to tag as you wish.

As an alternative you can find the hashtags you can enable the search by the way on "Discover", as they are trends that emit the content of interest found on the aforementioned Discover.

Search and find a user on Tik Tok

A great way to find a user is through a Tik Tok video that you are watching at that moment, to start the following steps:

1. Once the video shows the content creator on the left, the content creator is located above the bubble where their profile picture appears.

2. The next step is to tap the bubble to enter the user's profile.

3. Alternatively, once you keep watching the videos you can tap the identifier that appears in Tik Tok in the corner.

Another way to log in to explore a user's content is through Discover:

1. Enter Discover through the menu bar.

2. In the upper part you can search for the user.

Once you are in the profile of a Tik Tok user, you can explore in depth all the content it offers, where you will find all the data that are part of the credibility of the account, in addition you will find many links to go to their social networks, to this is added the variant of a public profile that displays this data.

Tips to grow your brand on Tik Tok

The important thing for a brand to scale in a big way on Tik Tok is to follow the expert instructions below:

1. Set up your own channel and make sure you create the most appropriate profile according to the type of audience you are looking for.

2. Get a PRO account to have access to metric data.

3. Post videos about the brand to show a more human identity.

4. Make alliances with influencers to achieve a great impact and that the content can reach more people.

5. It is best to have timeless content.

6. Be part of the current trend so that the content is adjusted to the same so you can go viral.

7. To start with, the most important thing is to publish 3 or 5 videos a day, but keeping the quality above all.

8. Alternate the length of the videos so that the content can be varied.

9. Comment on other users' videos to reach a greater number of visibility.

10. It takes care of every aesthetic detail to give the best possible impression.

Controversies within the operation of Tik Tok

Social network analysts have offered certain conclusions about Tik Tok, where they highlight that it is a much more special platform than many think, because it has been catalogued as one of those that obtains the most information, and even this includes the personal data of the creators.

For this reason, there may be some degree of concern about feeling that kind of vulnerability, but Tik Tok's response has been to improve the security of its functions with an algorithm designed for this purpose, where they have exposed a clear commitment to protect the privacy of each user.

Although care must be taken by the user as to the type of information he/she shares, if any doubts arise, you need to take a calm approach and be aware of the following points:

What information does Tik Tok have about you, the application only has the data you provide when you create the account.

How Tik Tok uses the information of your personal data, within the conditions state that the use of your data are directed towards your benefit, to create the suggestion on that content that fits your interest, in addition to advertising that is compatible with the profile.

The data requested by this social network is the date of birth, email, phone number, a description for the profile, photograph or even personal video, data extracted from contests or surveys, and the like.

Once you associate Tik Tok with other social networks such as Facebook, Twitter, Instagram or Google, you grant equal authorization for Tik Tok to have this information found on these platforms.

The scope of Disco ver Tik Tok comes to meet the information of the websites you have visited, this also includes even the applications you have downloaded or purchased for the purpose of taking into account the interests.

The study of the social network extends over the IP address, along with the browsing history, which is joined by the providers for mobile services, this corresponds to an advertising use.

Even phone contacts and a list of Facebook friends are considered so that invitations can be made so that they can visit the platform with ease.

Each of the mentioned data is used to adjust the services and support to your needs, or are used in order to comply with their conditions, it is a suggestion to mark the interests of each user, it is a connection that they seek to establish to make users feel important.

Although you must take into account that the information is a protection for the social network itself, because it can bring to light a sign of abuse and limit all kinds of illegal activity, it is a way to ensure security for both parties and control remains hand in hand with users.

Tik Tok content restrictions

The action of the Tik Tok algorithm prioritizes the issue of visual security, so when you intend to get followers it is important that you do not overlook these restrictions as your content can be damaged by an oversight like this, since the platform performs a clear monitoring of the content broadcast in the feed.

A wide variety of videos that have a negative impact on the user will not be shown, much less when it is about a medical procedure that exposes some action too graphic, much less if the subject matter is illegal, without leaving aside the fight that is imposed on the SPAM and videos to increase traffic.

The Tik Tok platform is responsible for setting aside the videos that do not comply with such measures, the intention above all is to enact quality content, otherwise these negative effects are triggered, and if that were not enough, there is an option called "family safety mode".

The previous action of family security is designed for parents seeking to protect minors on some type of content that is suitable for their children, this type of security also fulfills the function of limiting who they can write to and who can not, and even the screen time is regulated by this option.

How to earn money in Tik Tok?

The Tik Tok platform is a great opportunity for an influencer to find the popularity sought on this digital plane and generate income, especially because the impact of a large community is enough motivation for brands to seek this opportunity to market and promote products or services.

The generation of money on this social network is becoming a reality, especially with the huge amount of downloads available in mobile application stores, so all kinds of projects include this environment to take advantage of its visibility, reaching the point of becoming a modern trend.

In principle this social network has not been created for this commercial purpose, but at the same time with the constant use it has become a very friendly platform for advertising, for this reason it can be considered as a great alternative, where the creation of content opens the door to sponsor a product or an offer.

The approach used to generate income is similar to that of YouTube, but over time certain methods have also been implemented that pursue this monetization result, as it is a platform like any other with a valuable possibility to earn money with creativity and consistency.

Although beyond knowing the following alternatives to get money, you can not forget the duty to create value, because the content itself should be presented as a reason to revisit your account that interest is what makes a community grow, you can start to implement these actions to grow and monetize:

Live broadcasting

The opportunity provided by the live broadcast, causes viewers to follow the content creator closely, because beyond the publications you can begin to shape that image as an influencer, also through these transmissions can motivate viewers to give virtual coins called "Coins".

In this sense Tik Tok is similar to Twitch, these are purchased through real transactions, in exchange for these donations content creators can reciprocate with a gift or also support other users, it is a great opportunity to awaken empathy and continue to relate.

In Tik Tok 80% of the total value of the transmissions is transferred to the influencer, it is not a huge fortune, but it is an incentive that can serve as a revenue stream to consider, it does not hurt to be inspired by this type of recognition or contribution.

Sponsor brands

In Tik Tok as in other social networks there is a high interest on the part of brands to promote a product or service, this is chosen by the brand according to the type of content that the influencer emits, if it has to do with their brand, also when they manage to demonstrate a clear interest in the content of value and the number of followers.

In addition to this, the demographic effect is a common action within the digital world, it is not new but it should be taken into account for what it represents, since making money through social networks is not as impossible as it is thought.

Learn how to live stream on Tik Tok

For many Tik Tok users, live streaming is still a great mystery, this function is present by the very nature of this platform where content is published in a short format, but also allows you to create a variety of formats to attract the audience.

The recording functions include live broadcasting, this is very little used due to lack of knowledge, but it is important to explore every factor of this alternative so that it can be on your side, that way it will be much easier to start generating greater visibility within this social network.

Once you have a Tik Tok account you can opt for this content transmission in real time, which adds an important interface that does not generate any problem, achieving the option of earning money, if you keep this desire alive you just have to have 1000 followers, being a factor for publications.

On the other hand, a requirement to broadcast live is to be over 16 years old. Once these two measures are fulfilled, the following steps are required to publish live:

Install the Tik Tok application, either Play Store or App Store. Launch the application and then log in with your personal information.

Once you are in the application, click on the "+" icon at the bottom and then go to the "Live" button next to the "Record" button.

Then you can include your preferred title for the live broadcast, it is important to be creative to attract more followers.

When adding the title, it is necessary to add the "Broadcast live" button, so that the retransmission can start immediately. Once these steps have been completed, the live transmission starts in Tik Tok, at the end of the session you only have to click on "End live", then you can return to the home screen, managing to start the attempt to receive donations from your followers as mentioned above.

To materialize this way of obtaining money, you just need to know and use these steps, although the operation of regular donations is different, since the followers cannot send that money directly to the bank account, but a tip is sent through the coins that have been acquired through cash.

By having a significant amount of coins, they can be converted into diamonds, then transformed into real money via PayPal, for that Tik Tok withdrawal you need a balance of $100, this can be a slow process but with a busy following it is a valid option to consider.

Once you can put your talent to work in Tik Tok you can take advantage of every moment to generate money, this social network is an ideal way to show all kinds of skills, in addition to other actions that lead you in a great way towards obtaining profits:

Get the first 1000 followers:

For the Tik Tok platform to generate income it is necessary to have 1000 followers, that is the requirement for live recordings, so you need to upload content constantly to become a recognized character, it is better to reach and exceed that figure.

Don't lose track of the direct

It is necessary that every profile can count on live videos, either once or several times a week this is an important measure, the frequency depends on you and your goals, the more the better to build an image, but issuing a high value content to respond to followers with the best.

Move Tik Tok followers to other social networks

Once you have a large number of followers or at least a considerable one, it is best to diversify and gain strength on other social networks, this is useful for Instagram or any type of YouTube channel, thus becoming a crucial point to monetize easily and even opting for more economic models.

Get gifts with great charisma

While you are making your transmissions it is important to infect users with trending topics and great content, so they will be happy to make gifts within which highlight the stickers that can be used on the video, within the gifts sprout the options of obtaining real money as a donation.

Praise users

The motivation to have donations is essential to present a better emotion, so that all those who follow you can make donations as a kind of gift, and once they occur it is positive to respond with gratitude through live chats to highlight the praise.

How to watch live streaming videos with Tik Tok?

Beyond the function of live streaming, there is another doubt about viewing this type of content, before any difficulty of this type you only have to cover the following steps:

Log in to the Tik Tok application from your device.

Click on the "Notification" button near the "+" icon.

Once you are on the "Notifications Page", you can find the "Best Lives" option that appears at the top of the screen.

Tap the "Watch" button next to "Best Lives" to start playing the stream that has been made live via Tik Tok and randomly pops up.

The "Best Lives" feature allows you to browse through each content, and then on the notifications you can access the "main live video gallery", being a great opportunity to watch live broadcasts.

On the other hand, when you search for a particular user you have access to live broadcasts, the availability of this content is presented with a red circle on their profile picture, so you can have contact with such live content without any problem.

Discover how to advertise on Tik Tok

The ads started to be part of Tik Tok since 2019, the first time this feature made its appearance was by Chris Harihar, being one of the partners of Crenshaw Communications, it was about 5 seconds long ads, but in the platform other kind of advertising formats are presented as the following:

Brand acquisition

The ads that are carried out through acquisition are about the use of still images, videos and also GIFs, these can be linked directly on the website, it even works great on the challenges or challenge within Tik Tok itself, when you want to measure your reach of this strategy these metrics help:

Impressions.

Unique scope.

Clicks.

Native video

Native videos are used as important ads that make an impact and are measured under the following actions:

Engagement: By receiving likes, shares and comments.

Impressions.

Average playback duration.

Clicks.

Video display time: More than 3 seconds of playback, 10 seconds and also completion are required.

CTR.

Total video views.

On the other hand, video campaigns can be designed to have a close impact, the same happens with individual videos, the difference is on the duration, since Tik Tok videos last up to 15 seconds, while native videos last between 9 and 15 seconds, they are full screen ads.

As with Instagram and its ads present in stories, they can be skipped, an ad of this type can cover a lot of objectives behind a single option, as it can lead directly to the download of applications and can also get clicks on your website.

Branded lenses

The operation of the AR lenses are traced from Snapchat and Facebook, the same happens with Tik Tok, although its appearance is temporary, it fulfills a certain time and a particular function that has not yet been offered in its maximum expression, to continue completing the variety of functions of Tik Tok.

Winning content for Tik Tok

The popularity of a topic within Tik Tok can be investigated in advance to follow existing trends, starting from the most important categories such as educational orientation, fun, relationship or friendship, health topics, food and especially dance, to the point of reaching motivational content.

As if that were not enough, there are two very important areas within social media, such as beauty and crafts, finding the ideal path for your goals is an important step, the better and faster you can identify them, the more you will achieve that a content can have an important reach.

Finding and also creating themes to produce Tik Tok content is a task that works to postulate an active scene, this works so that a niche can have a development that is relevant today, plus you can anticipate original ideas about that area to be above.

The best thing about creating your own content is that you get to gather all the attention, in addition to this you gain a great personalization on an account, since it is an application where originality is a key requirement, so you can boost a presence of another level, being very useful for your brand, and to create campaigns.

The tip to impact with great success is to align directly with the planned, not to miss the opportunity to be part of the trend, also you can not try too hard in a creation of ingenuity, but it is best to rely on the safe, the simpler and brighter the video is achieved highlight this application.

How can you gain followers on Tik Tok?

Popularity within a social network is everything, so in Tik Tok you need an extra boost to gain presence, in principle one of the main strategies for this is the use of hashtags appropriately according to the content, this is part of a planning to define the target audience and reach them.

To move up within this platform it is vital to show content to the public interested in this topic, in addition to the obligation to be constant to nurture each user with a great proposal that can fit their tastes, it is based on achieving to earn that kind of appreciation within the digital world.

The organic reach is presented by achieving to present certain viral videos, to achieve this type of measure you just need to implement the following guidelines, beyond any trick this contributes on your content:

Constancia

It is important that at the moment of publishing a high frequency of at least 3 or 5 videos can be maintained, but where quality is the priority, because this prevails over quantity, at the beginning we recommend 2 to 3, from this starting point there are many possibilities of success.

Niche

The main focus in the midst of Tik Tok's trajectory is to form an ideal niche, since it is the environment in which to publish content of great value, where the fun side can not be lost for any reason, but can strengthen the sector, everything goes hand in hand with the theme to which you dedicate yourself.

Valuable content

It is much more special to have a section for your own content, this is the right way to establish your own style that will make you grow for what you offer, where the essence to maintain above all is a totally striking action that is established as a magnet for a larger audience.

Create an active account

It is important that within the growth of the account you can respond to each of the comments so that the interaction is kept well cared above all, this type of attention is highly valued and helps the rest of the people can connect with your content.

Own audios and creativity

In order to offer first class content you need to integrate ingenious actions such as an audio that comes from your ideas, this type of personalization provides great fun to the audience because in the end it is an ideal social network for others to have a great time.

Keys to success in Tik Tok

When you register in Tik Tok you can enter the ads section and make the most of this tool, in addition to the expert inspection of valuable content to achieve impact to the entire audience in a positive way, the goal of covering this social network requires enough dedication to bet on everything high.

Ads can be integrated from the feed itself, being a common action in both Facebook and Instagram, so it is possible to integrate an ad so that a strategy and commercial attraction can be developed, in addition to a great impression from the conformation of the account with the use of applications and bots.

Creating quality content is a breakthrough to reach personalized audiences, especially when the ads do not need too much investment, in fact the space can be bid and pay-per-click modules are what every user needs to scale in large magnitudes.

When using Tik Tok it is important to extend its functions to the maximum, so the best key is to learn how to record in the best way, using tricks and other skills you can record first class videos carefully to meet the main dynamics of this social network, the most important are the following:

Zoom in during recording

Use in your favor the zoom button is an advantage that is on this application, you only need to move the record button to the center of the screen, thus the action of the camera to apply the zoom on the image is issued to provide that effect that both aspire to implement.

Switch between rear and front camera

You only need to double tap on the screen to easily switch cameras, the important thing is that each video can be well taken care of with a high level of quality, as long as you can fully test the speed and performance of your camera you will get great footage and enjoyment.

Turn a Tik Tok video into a Gif

If you want to share a Tik Tok video in the form of a Gif to gain greater disclosure, you only need to go over the video to achieve touch the share option, then in the last option of the application you must select the alternative to share as Gif, you can also choose the footage and it is saved in the gallery.

How to make a video viral on Tik Tok?

In order to get a video to make the best possible buzz and impression on Tik Tok so that many people talk about your content, you should take into account the following points:

You need users to see your video through the "for you" section so they can follow you.

The content must be reproduced several times.

Share the video to gain comments and likes.

The ideal length for a video to go viral is a short one of at least 15 seconds, it causes better sensations than one of 60 seconds.

Once you can comply with these points you will make your account and content go viral, at first it may seem complicated but it is an easy path with dedication so you can make it go viral, it is important that it can cause a positive impact to be shown to more people.

Tik Tok analyzes the impact of your account when generating or providing viral content, so if you have a PRO account it is easier to find the metrics you need to boost, the most important is the comment, views and shares, winning in one of these three elements can be considered as viral.

How to use hashtags in Tik Tok?

The hashtags that belong to Tik Tok work the same as in other social networks, these are interesting for representing the theme of your content, its use fulfills the function of achieving greater reach, this means to be more responsive to the audience is ideal, to be viral above all.

It is important that within the selection of these words you can find a concrete relationship because it is the way to reach the public, so that everything is in order, the following actions must be covered:

The use of hashtags in Tik Tok is a great help to give a clear category to the content, the important thing is that the videos are within reach of the audience you are trying to reach.

Look first and foremost to add the hashtags to the videos by pronouncing those same words for a full connection, thereby coming to be considered as a niche.

Gain power by creating your own hashtags so that the user can become infected and participate by using them.

Use hashtags that are active to have the effect of a greater reach.

Take into account the song you use because they are linked to certain hashtags.

Temporary hashtags obey to events or some kind of challenges, so you can create your own to take advantage of that kind of commotion in favor of your own campaign.

You need to research hashtags beforehand to use the ones that are trending, as well as locate your competition and observe what they are doing.

It is important to maintain a balance with the use of hashtags, because when you abuse the content loses value, everything must be applied with sense, as long as it has to do with the content there will be no problem, there are many tools to find the most current for your category and get positioned along with the trend.

How to use TikCode to increase followers?

The options and amplitudes of Tik Tok do not stop growing to present a great scenario to obtain a high level of popularity, that is why this application offers the function of using TikCode in that way you can share a user in a better way, that is why it is important to know how to implement this alternative.

To get other people to follow you, the TikCode option is a great action to exhaust to reach the expected level, this facilitates not having to give or issue a user to know you, you only have to share the code assigned to your account to be scanned and thus reach more people to your account.

The TikCode is a code that is issued in a personalized way, through this way you can share this type of presentation so that others can follow you, it is a great way to make yourself known, and left in the past the action of writing or entering text, for this reason you only have to point the device to the code.

The operation of TikCode works in a similar way to the inclusion of the QR code, so when a scan occurs, immediately the profile appears so that they can follow you in Tik Tok, this type of way is much more effective and others can not waste time but follow you directly.

The benefits of using TikCode

The use of TikCode generates important advantages in order to take full advantage of this application, the most specific effects are the following:

There is no risk in sharing the TikCode that they will be mistaken or there will be confusion when following you.

You don't need to dictate or type your user name.

You can download this code to print it and use it as a cover letter in any circumstance.

With the image of the code you can share it on social networks.

This type of code is a quick presentation and only takes a few minutes.

In Instagram in the same way you can create a QR code in the way you aspire to achieve customize your identity to social media, to do so with the TikCode should only be used as profile picture this is installed automatically, the presence in each social network is very important.

To use this code you must create a quick access through the Tik Tok account, to enter the "Me" section, this arises from the application profile, then in the application settings, on the lower right corner you must touch those three dots to open the settings and privacy section to go to TikCode.

When you perform these settings steps you can see your TikCode which is located next to your profile picture, then at the bottom you have the options to save the QR code or also scan, once you manage to save the code you can download the TikCode as an image in your own gallery.

How does the Tik Tok algorithm work?

The operation of Tik Tok arouses great curiosity and attention on many users, especially if you are looking to conquer popularity within this medium, so you need to apply certain tricks to learn more about the users that make up this platform. Tik Tok's algorithm is very similar to that of other social networks, although it has certain innovative features, since most platforms take into account the likes of each profile according to the interactions and the type of accounts they follow, but in the case of Tik Tok it is different.

Tik Tok's method is based on the user's experience, so they have focused on perfecting searches, where the main interest is to know each user closely, but their review includes search engines to find the preferences behind the content and interactions.

Since each user makes a comment or follows a user, an input is generated for the system to detect what you like, this is part of knowing this social network to make the most of its functions as a tool, the incursion on its algorithm is important.

The difference over the dynamics of other social networks is based on taking into account other kinds of factors, this is because they analyze other kinds of data, seeking to deepen on the tastes of each user, it is much more than knowing a profile, the intention is to omit the information that does not motivate any reaction on the feed.

The main novelties that emerge about the functioning of the Tik Tok algorithm are the following considerations:

The interaction that each user presents with the videos he/she likes and shares: the system tracks these actions and even if the user reaches the end of the video or just looks for the next one, to generate a ranking on the content that is ideal for your interest.

The comments made by a user: Tik Tok before each interaction gets to know better all kinds of users to have the advantage of finding the content you want to see quickly, it acts as a kind of personalization.

In the case of user-generated content: The social network is responsible for classifying each of the interests based on content, style and even design, everything that is published in the feed is considered as a kind of identity of the user.

Video information: The platform performs a deep study on all the details of the video, within which subtitles, hashtags, and also sounds are considered, all these elements can make you stand out within this social network, it is necessary to dedicate attention to it.

Device and account settings: Language data about the account and the country you are on, along with the device you use, become considered through Tik Tok's algorithm, although it is not as determinant as other types of factors.

The Tik Tok platform also issues certain studies to consider, because it manages to detect repetitive patterns, this is because the main thing that the social network seeks is to keep boredom away on users, so this is a great advantage that is installed to intersperse the content in a better way by understanding what the user loves.

The main movement of this social network causes that you will not see repeated content, much less videos without sound, as if that were not enough, within the feed excludes all kinds of content that you have already viewed, or any other that is classified as SPAM, it is an empathy to prioritize the fun.

The focus of this social network is based on keeping each user attached to the platform, it also provides a perspective to have contact with more experiences, the proportion of new ideas and different types of creators is the main theme.

Master the Tik Tok algorithm

The magic formula to obtain better positioning on the Tik Tok algorithm is the following estimations:

Get more and more likes.

Generate more comments.

Publish first before other similar content.

To have more followers.

Insert sounds that are genuine or original.

Understanding this measure controls the operation of this social network to achieve the expected success, although other additional factors may intervene such as the user's history, the actions of the device and also the location, it is a personalized measure, but on the platform the most important thing is to get likes.

In the face of some trend there may be a tie on a video, and the way to highlight one from another is through the comments, the rest is to consider the number of followers, in addition to the filter of a language, the factor to consider is the measure of the number of videos among the content that you can create.

As long as the sound is original, it will always be positioned in first place, that is why it is an environment completely dedicated to creativity, since the more you can innovate, the better results you end up producing, this is an opportunity although these rules can be broken with videos with the label of official.

Ideal tricks for your Tik Tok videos

Beyond the basic operation of Tik Tok, it is valuable for you to know tricks that open up all the alternatives to cover all that the social network offers, where the following points stand out:

How to record duets in Tik Tok

A very attractive modality within social networks is a duo, every user that can offer this type of interaction provides a better impact, especially when it is done through a collabora-tion with an influencer, everything consists of recreating a video that has dialogues, so that the other person can assume the other role.

This type of action or content can effectively go viral, although it is necessary to have access to the videos that have the option to enable duets, thus presenting a much more fun impression, and the followers of both accounts can find this type of content to grow together.

How reactions develop in Tik Tok

Within the important variety of functions of Tik Tok are the reactions, this is a way to interact that connects many users, this is done through a simple click to achieve press the share option that is right in the section where the "react" option appears to record the comment.

How transitions are used

One of the trendy elements within Tik Tok are the transitions, one of the effects that caused hallucinations on anyone is the famous "change of clothes", all thanks to the fact that this social network allows in a second to obtain this type of effect in a simple way, all this is developed by means of the timer.

To record over the same clip what you have to do is to keep the device in the same position, and then start recording the next video when you change clothes, keeping the same previous position, that way you can play and explore with the transitions, this and much more can be done from Tik Tok.

All the variety of effects is first class so that each brand or personal objective gets a much more creative vision, it is a dynamic way to present yourself to the world in style, it is a different action to show an exclusive content and that can win the audience's liking.

How to upload your own audio on Tik Tok

When publishing content in Tik Tok you have the option to insert your own audio without any problem, this type of originality is very well received by the application, it helps to climb to a better rate of traffic, so it is an important action to have the kind of visibility you need, you just have to carry out these steps:

Record a video in Tik Tok through your voice.

Place the video in private.

You can start the video recording again, but you must go to the private video that has your voice, and you can start using it freely.

You must assign a name to the voice because this way you can position it in Google to have more interaction.

Learn how to perform dubbing

The operation of Tik Tok with dubbing is interesting to conform all kinds of scenes, where the first key step is to learn very well what you plan to simulate so that you can then take care of vocalizing it freely, as long as you have in mind the dialogues you will not have any problem.

It is better to use a slow speed for the sound, so that when it is published you will get a view at normal speed and you will be at the same pace as the original audio, that way nothing can be missed, it is simple but very effective this type of alternative, so you do not give up this interaction.

How to integrate text into your motion videos

The best thing about Tik Tok is that within its functions or options you can easily add texts, these can disappear and appear without problems, this customization adjusts to the rhythm of the music freely, once it is recorded, select the "A" icon to organize it on the video, and when you hover over the dialogues you can choose the duration.

How to add voice-over to your videos

One of the cool effects that Tik Tok offers is the option to freely record your voice over, this integration causes a video to get a great outcome, it is compatible for tutorials, explanations and any type of graphic scene that needs a sound accompaniment.

How to adjust and edit a video within Tik Tok

When using Tik Tok it is important that you can forget about external applications, since everything is integrated on its options, among which is the editing of clips, with an important variety of filters, is part of the offer of this social network.

Check list before uploading a video

The previous steps to achieve that a video is just as you aspire and with a great visibility are very important, within which the following measures stand out:

Integrate a music before recording the video, the expected duration is 15 seconds, otherwise it will be cut.

It is important that the texts inserted in the video can occupy a central or lateral area that cannot overshadow the content, the important thing is that it reads well.

Inspect the copy that is part of the video, after being published this cannot be edited and generates more inconveniences.

Use around 3 to 6 hashtags so that the video can get the expected reach and visibility.

It is important to integrate the cover with the video to draw attention to the feed.

It features phrases as calls to action to gain comments and interaction.

Limitations present in Tik Tok

Before being part of Tik Tok it is essential to know in depth the steps or actions that you can not pass to avoid problems; the first thing is that you can only follow 200 accounts per day, you can not add two sounds on the same video, in some cases the effects vary for each type of account and you can only 500 likes per day.

Uses music sponsored by Tik Tok

When you are looking to find an account with a greater reach, it is important to find audios sponsored by Tik Tok, this type of audios have a blue icon that means that they are sponsored, this is the best way to gain visibility.

The best applications to get followers on Tik Tok

The appearance of applications to gain followers in Tik Tok has a lot to do with all the commotion that this social network has generated, but it is important to know which are the most effective or the fake ones, so you do not waste time and can grow as you aspire within this social network.

Nowadays there are a great number of applications to grow exponentially in Tik Tok, the methods have diversified every day, the important thing is to take as a main requirement that you get real followers, and without having to pay, these are two estimates to consider.

It is important to take into account that many applications provide temporary followers, so it is a primary help that needs to be reinforced with attention and consistency not to be neglected, so you have a profile and an attendance that will lead you on the right path within this social network.

Within the Play Store there are thousands of options for Android applications, so to save you bad experiences on this social network you can choose from the following alternatives the one that best meets your needs:

New BoostLike

This application works in English but this will not be a problem since its options are easy to use, this is due to the fact that the interface is intuitive and responds to your needs, thanks to its functions you can increase the number of followers and even the likes of the videos you make.

More than 50,000 users have downloaded and used this application, and it does not take up much space on your device as it weighs 4 MB, for this reason there are several facilities for the installation of the application, and it can be associated with several Tik Tok accounts at the same time to launch its functions.

Tik Booster fans

The operation of Tik Booster fans is ideal to increase the number of followers in Tik Tok, it is a totally free application that helps to gain likes and even have real fans so that you can create an ideal profile within this social network, additionally there is the function of getting comments on the videos. The dynamics of this application is based on a follow x follow, so you must follow users who are behind a list provided by the application, and this will instantly return the follow, it is an exchange to have a real audience to have a much more attractive profile.

Realfollowers.ly

In third place is Realfollowers.ly a very popular option within the community of Tik Tok users, this is because its operation is different, since it is responsible for performing and operating through an analysis on the account and that of each of your followers to issue hashtags recommendations.

When making a publication, you can use these tags to gain greater visibility among users and become an influencer, best of all is that no prior registration is required, not even required to provide more information about the account, it is safe and gives you strategies to become viral on this social network.

TikBooster

TikBooster is one of the most loved applications to get followers, in fact it leads the ranking of this type of applications in many websites, its functions are very simple to use, and it also has an integrated card game, through which you assign the number of fans you win and they are added to your account in just 24 hours.

To start with this application you only have to enter your username so that the application can assign to your account the new followers that you have gained, for this reason you do not run any risk, you can use this application with total security and it is fun for its fast operation.

TikFame

Within these Android applications, TikFame arises to support you to be famous within this social network, it allows you to gain up to more than a thousand real followers every day, its functions are totally free, in addition to the extension of recommendations for you to gain a higher level of popularity on this social network.

By using this application you can find the hashtags that best suit the theme of your content, this allows you to create better reactions to your videos and continue to climb in this social network, another kind of trick it has is the option to fake your statistics to have a more forceful profile.

TikLiker

TikLiker is one of the right applications to grow in Tik Tok, if you are looking to gain many "Likes" this is the medium you need, it also generates comments on the content you post on Tik Tok, in the case of gaining followers this option is activated through a game system that assigns your opportunities.

The use of this application is totally free, in the middle of the game you earn coins that allow you to carry out more functions such as the analysis of your profile, in addition to closely follow your profile to issue hashtags to improve the reach on this social network.

Vip Tools

A great application to have a large number of followers is Vip Tools, it has important functions and tools after a simple download, its mission is to give you more views, along with followers or likes, to this is added the option to get information about other users.

The implementation of this application is put into practice by simply entering the name of your user, to offer a large portion of information, then you can count on the action of following each of these users in one fell swoop or be even a little more selective, the options are at your disposal.

Is it safe to use applications to gain follo-wers on Tik Tok?

Most applications have a valuable level of security to use them and gain followers in Tik Tok, however the main pre-caution you should take is not to reveal your password for any reason, also when an advertisement or payment option appears it is important to check that it is official, most of them are free.

How to get more likes on Tik Tok?

To have the admiration and attention of more users on Tik Tok, you need to focus first and foremost on creating top-notch content, this way you can get a better charm on your followers, so you can start giving each user what they want, the more content the more likes on the posts.

Hack solutions to gain followers

To gain a higher level of presence on Tik Tok you can use certain third party tools that will help you reach the level you expect, these are the ones you should know and use:

Media Mister

Media Miser is an ally to generate a great presence on social media, each account can be enhanced with these functions, its services are directed towards users of Facebook, Instagram, YouTube and of course Tik Tok, its purpose is to get likes, followers and even analysis on the account.

You can find promotional services through this tool, being a great contribution to share the Tik Tok account on other social networks and gain traffic within your content, you should know this alternative to improve your presence within this social network and combine it with your valuable content.

TikTokFans

This is an option for you to improve the number of followers and also have that kind of tracking, its functions are free and provides statistics so that you can notice the number of followers live, where you can also compare the margin of what you have gained and the activity it generates.

Grabsocialer

Grabsocialer is postulated as a website that gives you support to gain a greater number of followers, but it is also a dedicated marketing service hosting for social media, this platform for free provides extensive assistance to not leave aside the duty to capture good content.

Trollishly

It is a tool dedicated to the improvement of followers within Tik Tok, it has a great choice of packages so you can choose the one that best suits your needs, in less than an hour you can start enjoying the best features to grow exponentially on this social network.

The Social Grower

The Social Grower is a site designed to help you get more relevance on your account, that level of popularity you are looking for is on this website that has important consulting services to also find solutions on web design and marketing.

SocialPromoter

The SocialPromoter alternative is in charge of offering tricks so that users can increase the number of likes on Tik Tok with total freedom, this online service source is a great alternative to carry out marketing strategies to monetize videos.

Tiktok Guru

Using Tiktok Guru is an ideal trick that you can employ to boost your climb to more followers, its operation is totally online and you won't have to make any download, so you can buy likes or have access to the subscription that fits your needs.

SMMPortal

It is an instrument in charge of driving you to gain followers, in addition there are several packages that you can buy to use it as a kind of reinforcement over the other social platforms, the essential thing is that you can take care of your presence in every way.

Where to buy likes, followers and views for Tik Tok

The options to buy that interaction you need to grow in Tik Tok are very diverse and you need to have more security for it, this way you can take advantage of the traffic generated by an application that is part of the global trend, so you can enjoy the breadth of this platform for your brand.

Tik Tok is an app that is worth investing in, it's passing Facebook, Instagram and Twitter, and it's simpler because it's a video sharing service, it opens up a great opportunity to be creative and grow a commercial message or your own career as an influencer.

BBC data show that this social network yields an annual income of $26 to $32,000, so it is a profit that becomes a great attraction for it is a great option to invest by buying likes, views and followers, these are basic actions that make you take off to the best sense.

But the entertainment effect also becomes attractive, along with the option to generate money, but for that you need to work and opt for all means to climb towards a large amount of "likes", views and followers, that is the formula for you to get more presence and you can invest in it through these options:

TokSocial

The TokSocial alternative is a great way for you to find services that do not spam, with this action you will not have to worry about fake followers, all thanks to the fact that only real accounts will follow your account, for this reason it is a paid tool that generates guarantees.

Social Tik

This tool guarantees that you will continue to grow within this social network, you can scale another level with the results of presence that provides, also you will not have to worry about any doubt, as they expose an unconditional support, this is coupled with a fast delivery system for you to continue growing in the world of this platform.

Viraholic

Viraholic's capability helps you to get another level of impression through its different service packages, these can be TikTok Starter, TikTok Influencer or TikTok Future Star, the prices are varied according to each function offered by these packages, so you can choose with comfort.

TokUpgrade

A great recommendation to find likes, views and followers on Tik Tok is TokUpgrade, this is a great platform for marketing, it is one of the best priced sites, you can find answers for your videos to level up and even expand your online audience.

Leo Boost

Leo Boost is one of the particular services because of its payment methods, since it does not have the availability with PayPal, but it is still a great option to retain more interaction, especially when you are looking to grow as an influencer, it is a good start for your channel to be ideal.

Musically Po

This company is not very well known in the market but when you are looking for cheap options this is the solution, since their costs start from $1.99 where services are managed quickly so that you have a feasible delivery, you should pay attention to this website to create an identity in Tik Tok,

Tik Tok breaks down any barrier

The operation of the application generates a high addiction especially in recent years, where it presents a high potential to be an ideal platform where you develop forms of marketing that fit your theme, and above all it is the presence in social networks that you need.

Tik Tok value content can turn you into a great influencer, as well as help a brand to scale to the level you expect, all thanks to the creative connection that occurs with each user directly, especially for the accompaniment that can be made with advertising products.

To reach more places in the world this social network is a brilliant alternative, where the main thing is to take into account your offer to explore the functions of this application, by creating this nexus, you can grow and monetize as soon as possible, where the essential thing is to keep the account crowded with content.

With so many emerging markets, it is important to consider this type of application, because your content can go viral with very little effort compared to the past, advertising has innovated at a high level with the inclusion of video, so as not to overwhelm the audience, but rather to be pleasant and achieve the expected effect.

Other titles of Red Influencer

Secrets for Influencers: Growth Hacks for Instagram and Youtube.

Practical Secrets to Gain Subscribers on Youtube and Instagram, Create Engagement and Multiply Reach.

Are you starting to monetize on Instagram or Youtube?

In this book you will find Hacks to increase your reach. Secrets for direct and clear Influencers such as:

Automate Instagram posts
How to generate traffic on Instagram, 2020 tricks
Instagram 2020 algorithm, learn everything you need to know.
Instagram tips to improve interaction with our followers
18 Ways to gain followers on Instagram for free
Learn with us how to monetize your Instagram profile
Key Websites to Get Followers on Instagram Quickly
Instagram 2020 Trends
2020 Guide: How to become a youtuber
How to become a Youtuber Gamer
2020 Hacks to get more subscribers on YouTube
Hacks to rank your YouTube videos in 2020
Hack for Youtube, Change Pause Button for Subscription Button

A book with which you will see both the general aspects and what it takes to make a living from the influencer profession.

We deal openly with topics such as buying followers, and hacks to improve interaction. BlackHat strategies at your fingertips, that most agencies or Influencers do not dare to recognize.

At Red Influencer we have been advising MicroInfluencers like you for more than 5 years to create their content strategy, improve their reach and impact in networks.

If you want to be an influencer, this book is a must. You will have to develop knowledge about platforms, strategies, audiences and how to reach maximum visibility and monetize your activity.

We have experience with Influencers of all ages and subjects, and you can be one too.

Get this book and start applying the professional secrets to Gain Followers and Become an Influencer.

This is a practical guide for intermediate and advanced level Influencers, who do not see the expected results or who are stuck.

Strategy and engagment are as important factors as the volume of subscribers, but there are Hacks to boost them, in this guide you will find many of them.

No matter if you want to be a Youtuber, Instagrammer or Tuitero, with these strategies and keys you will be able to apply them to your social networks.

We know that being an Influencer is not easy and we do not sell smoke like others, everything you will find in this book is the synthesis of many success stories that have gone through our agency.

Influencer Marketing is here to stay no matter what you say. And there are more and more brand ambassadors. People who, like you, started working on their personal brand and targeting a specific niche.

We unravel in detail all the secrets of the sector that moves millions!

You will be able to apply our tips and hacks to your Social Media strategies to increase CTR, improve loyalty and have a solid content strategy in the medium and long term.

If others have been able to monetize with perseverance, dedication and originality, you can too!

In our platform redinfluencer.com we have thousands of registered users. A contact channel through which you can offer your services in a markeplace of reviews for brands, and which will receive offers to your email periodically.